This Book Belongs To:

First edition: 2018

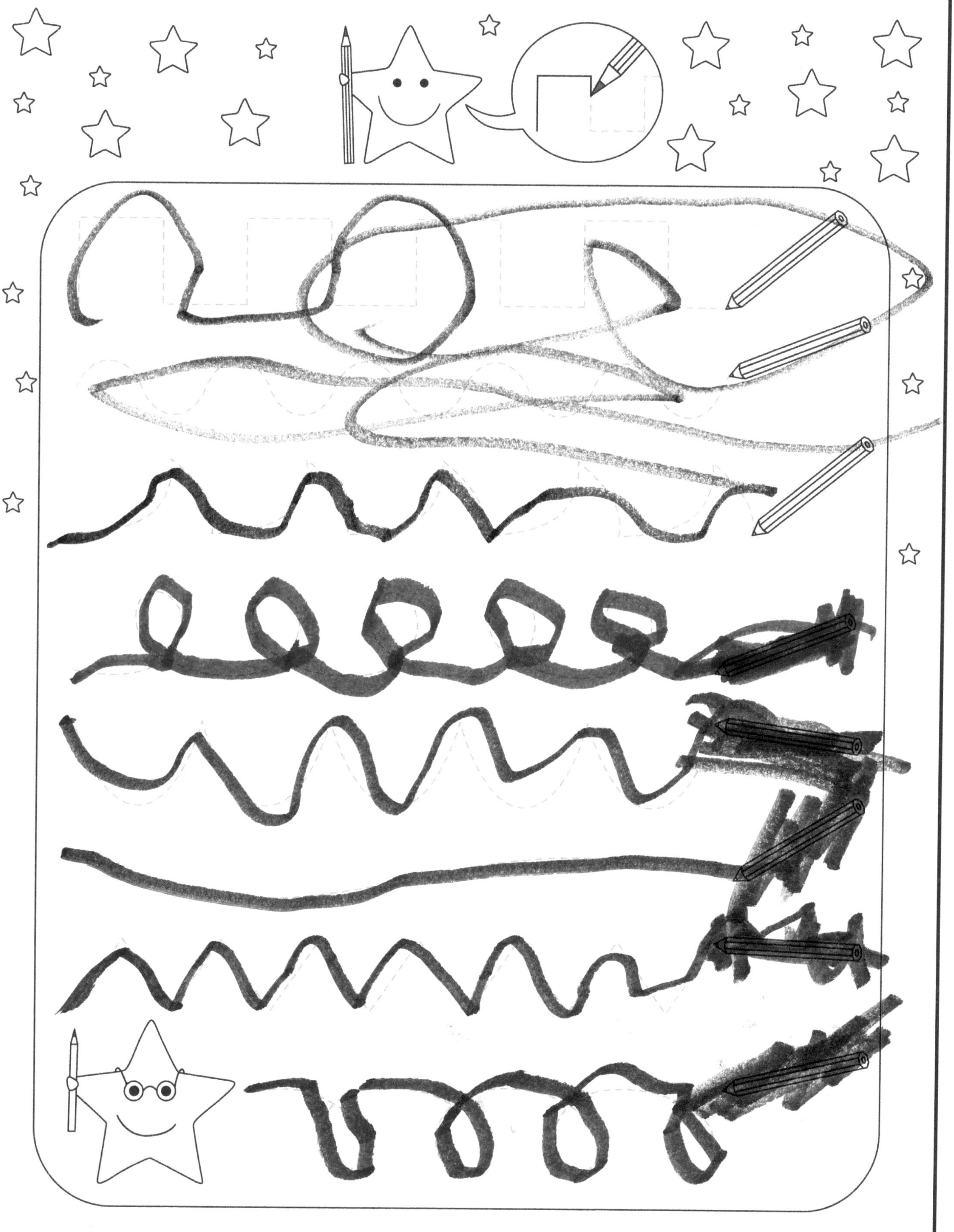

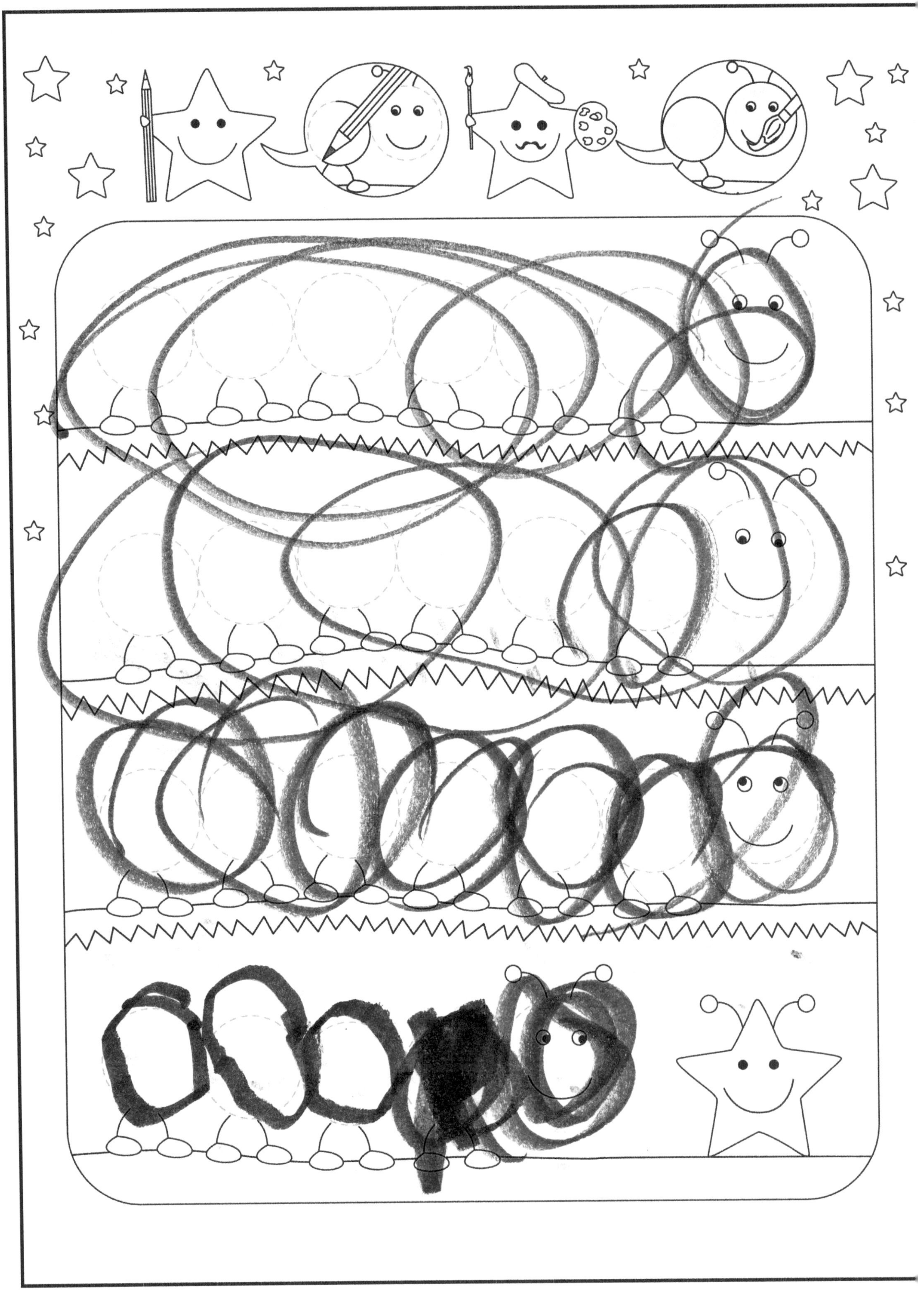

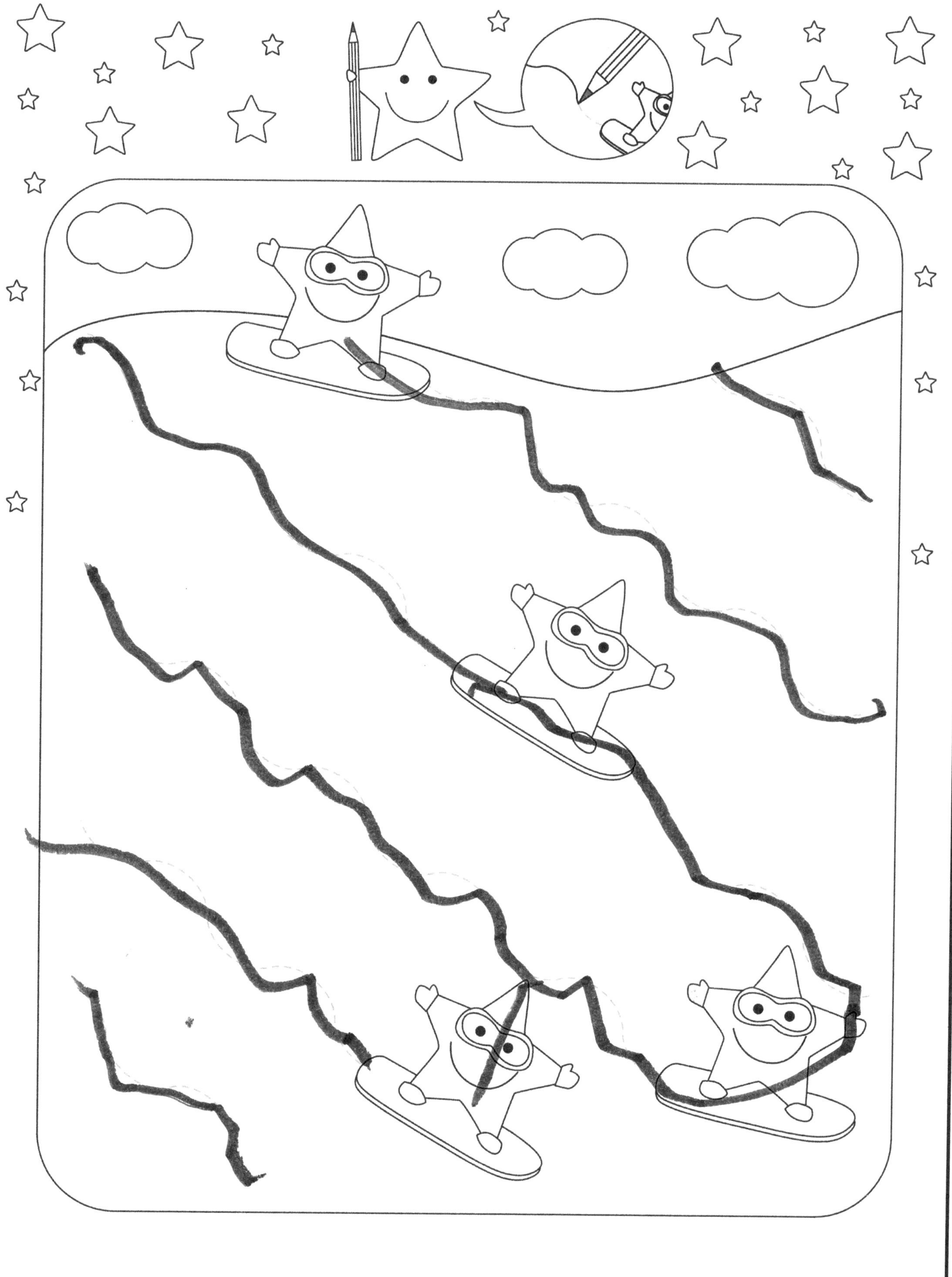

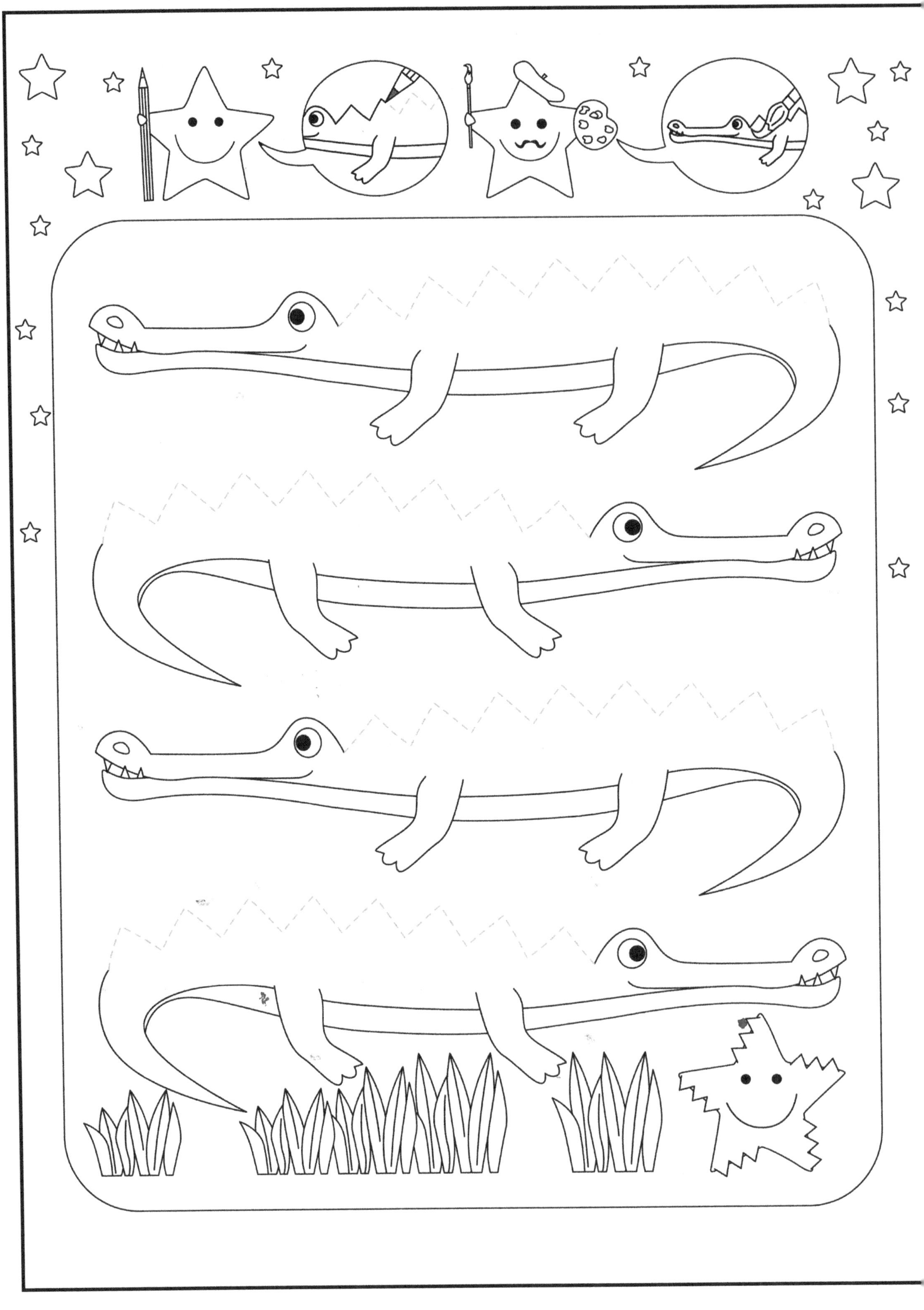

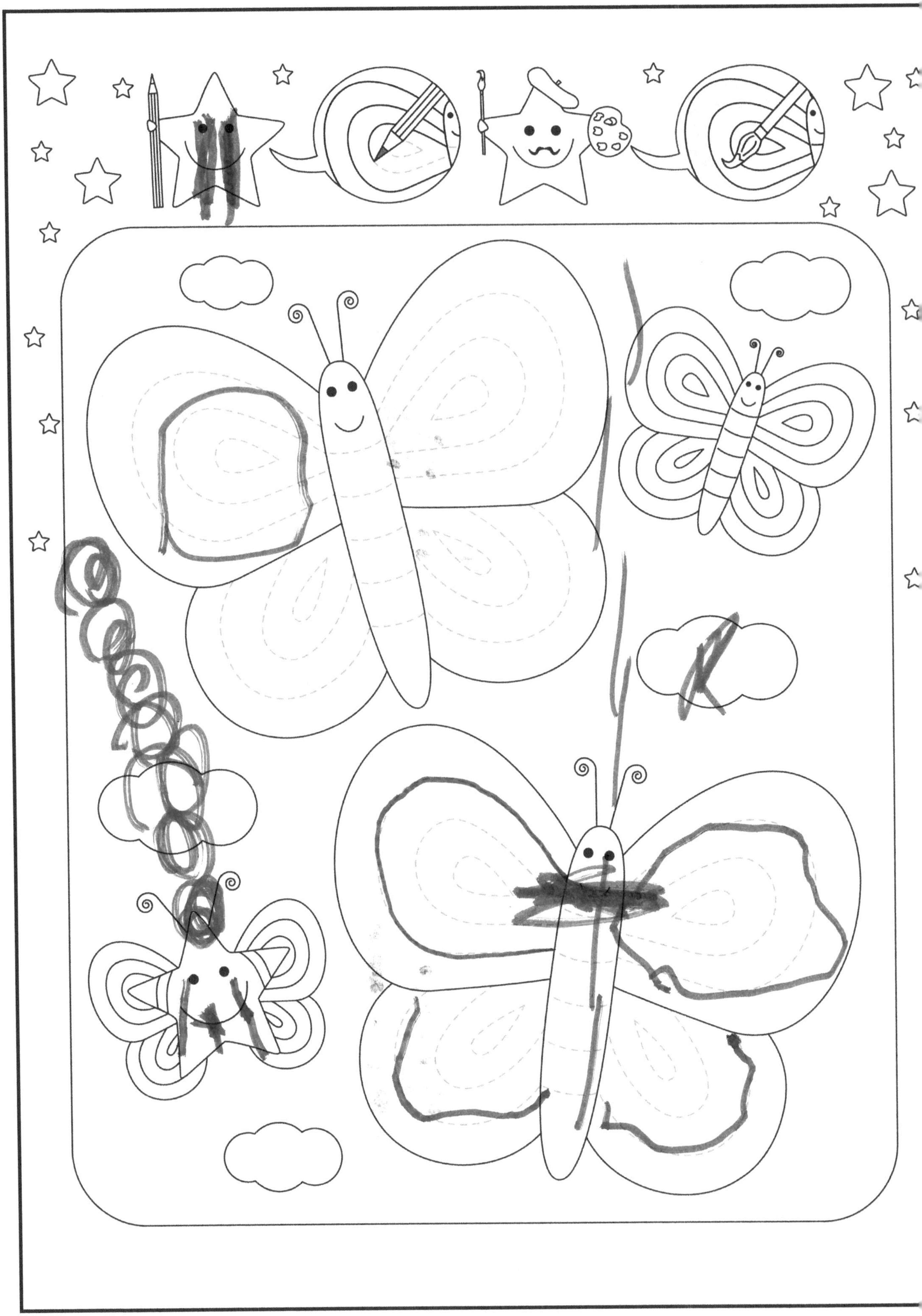

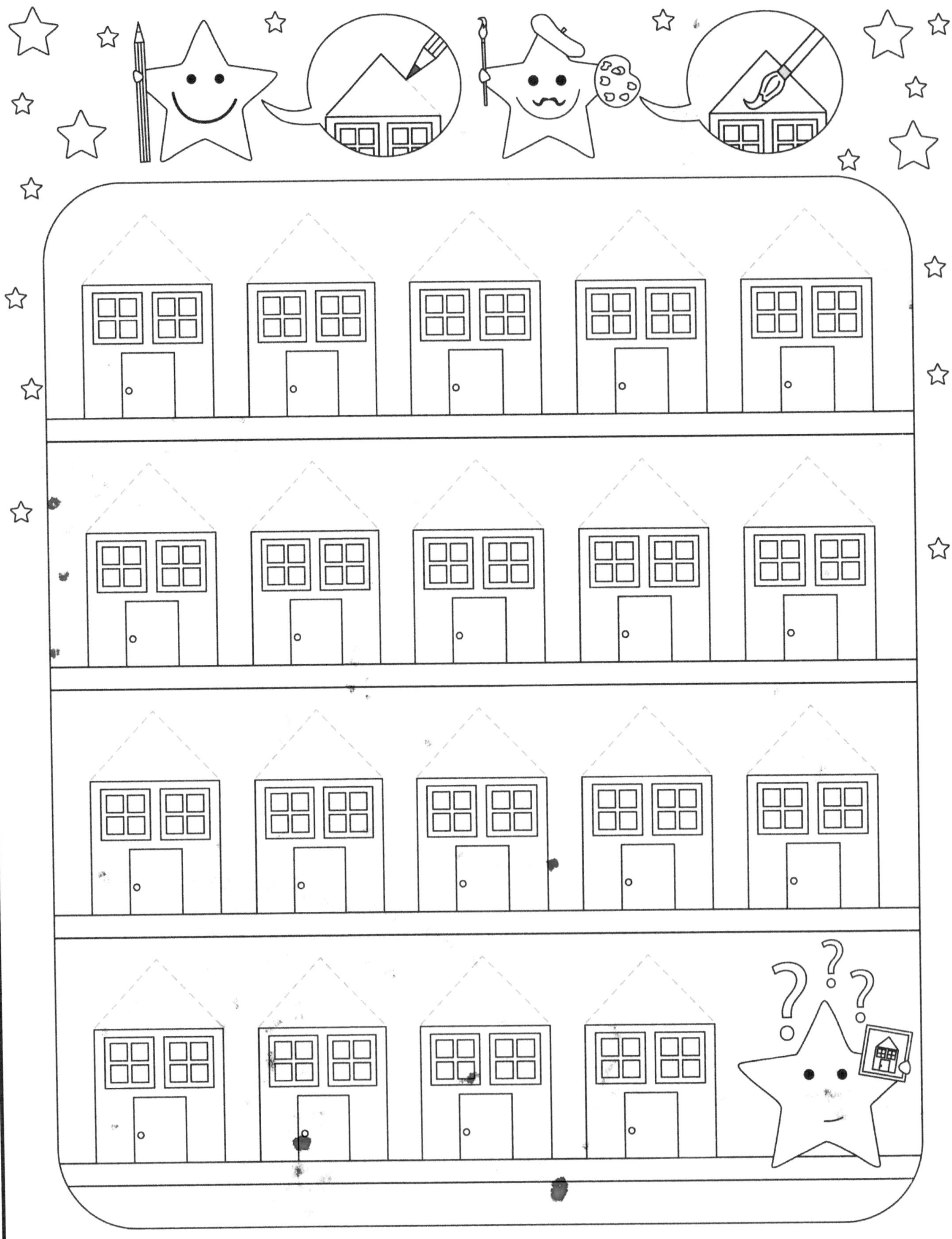

zzzZZ

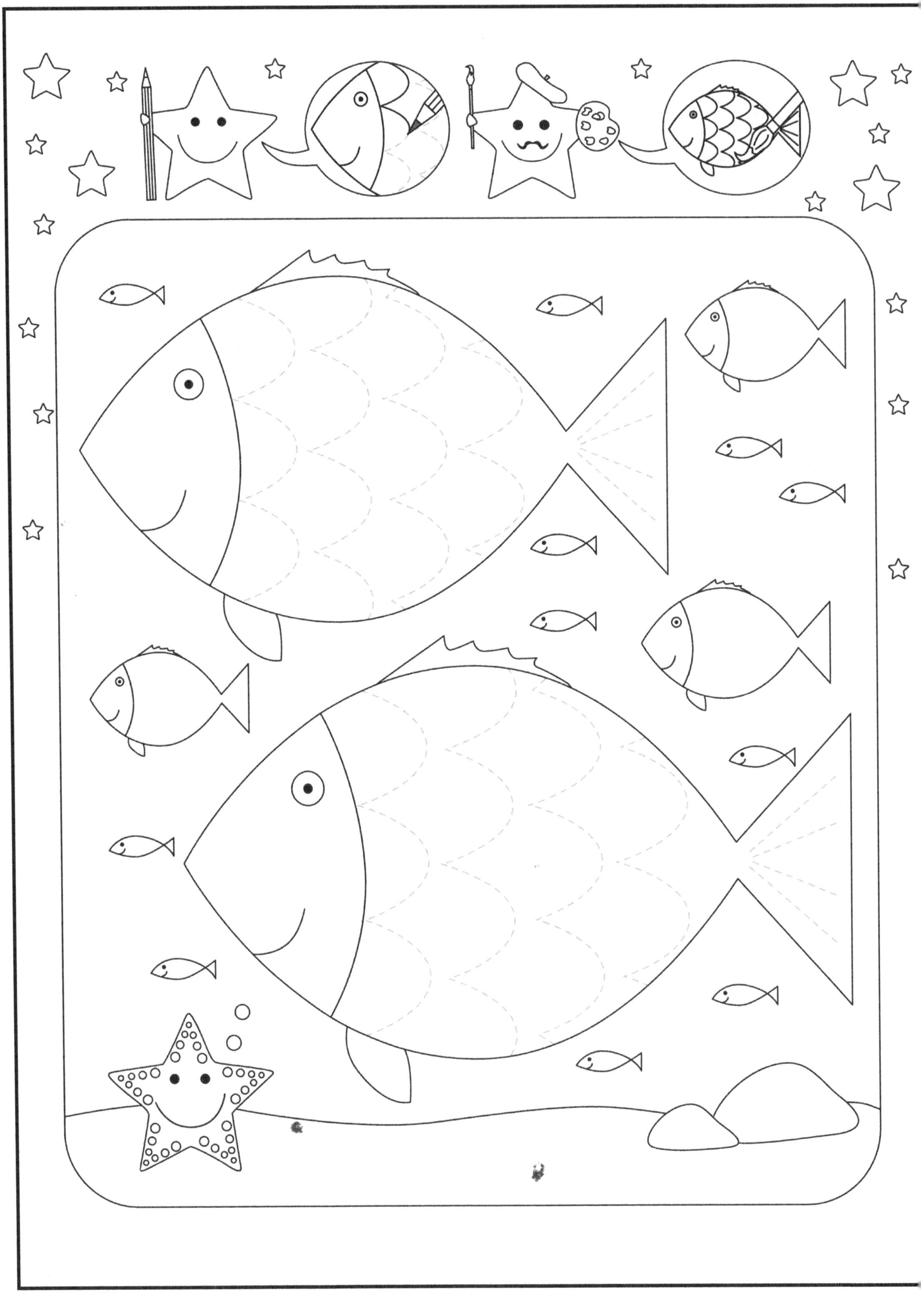

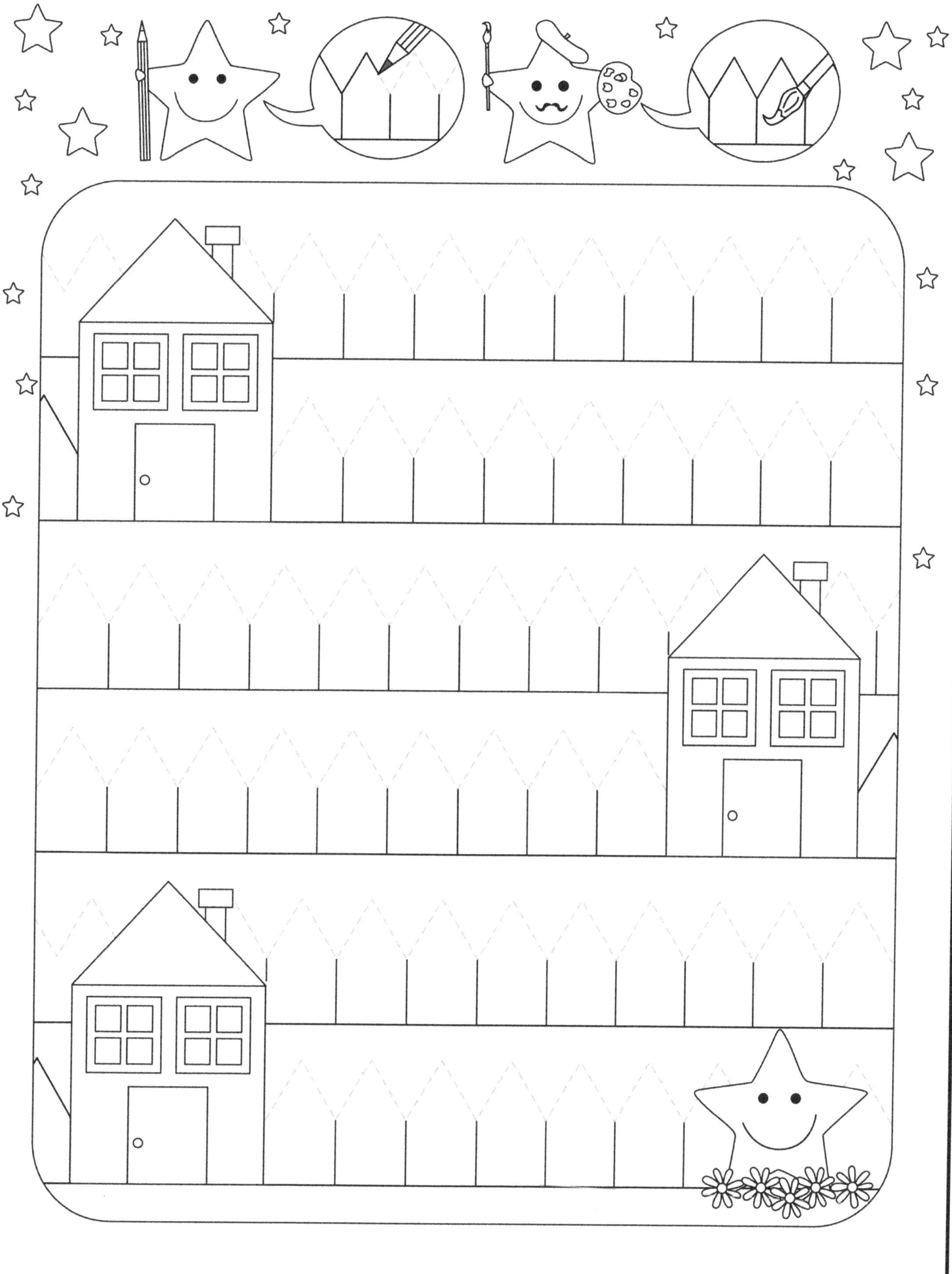

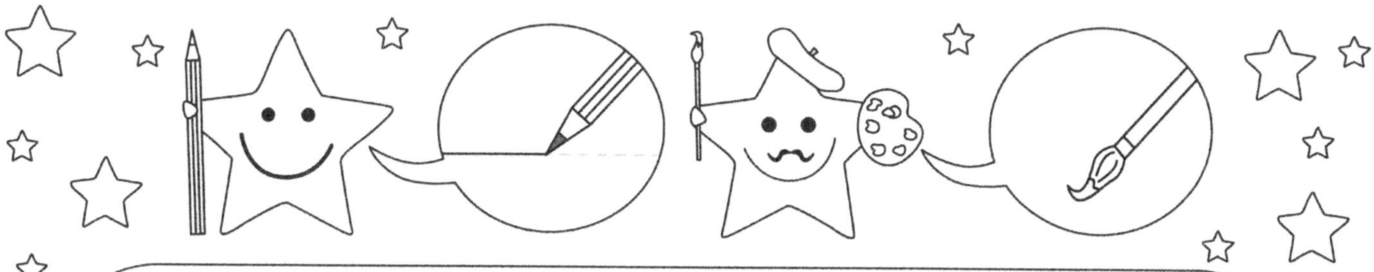

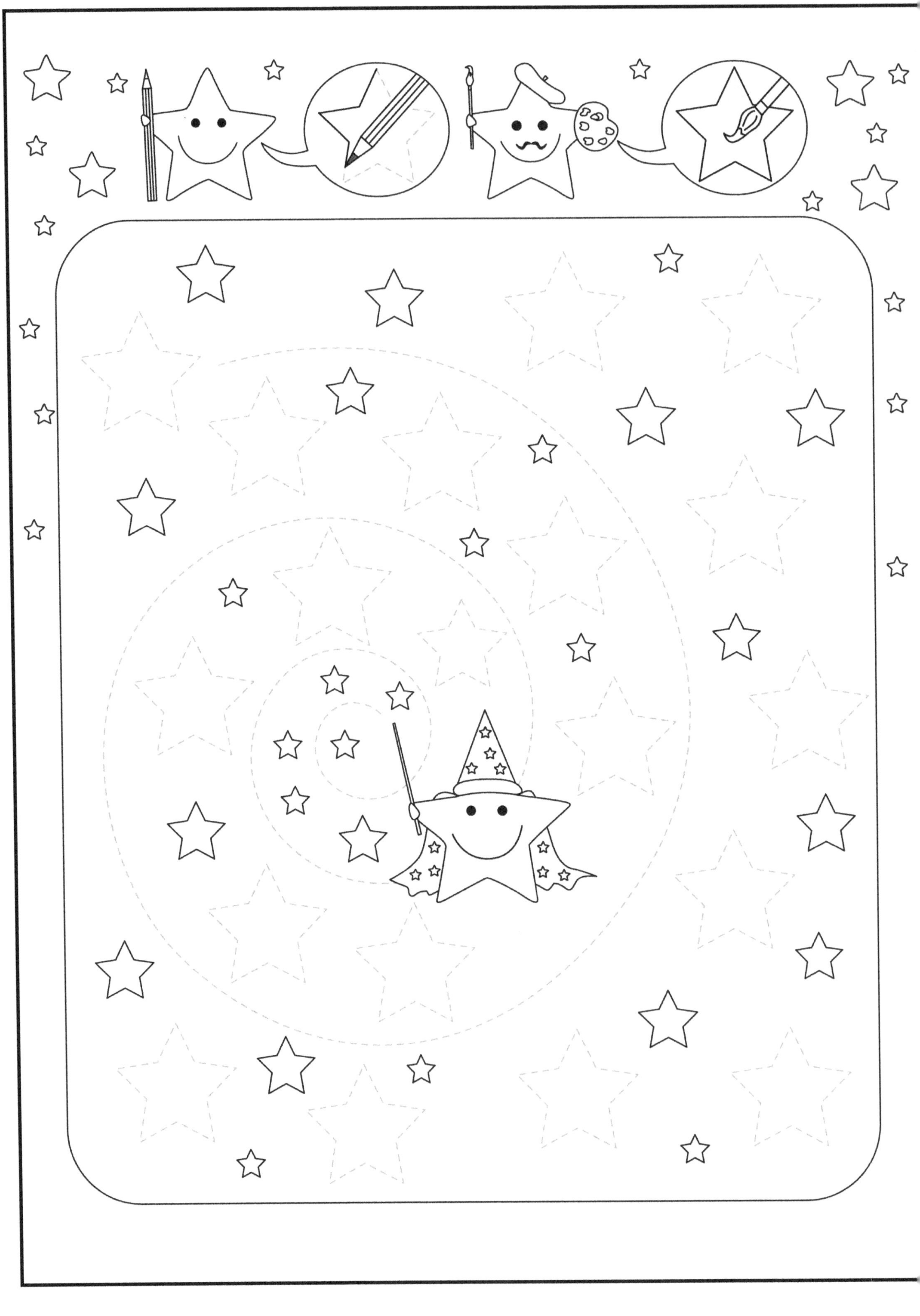

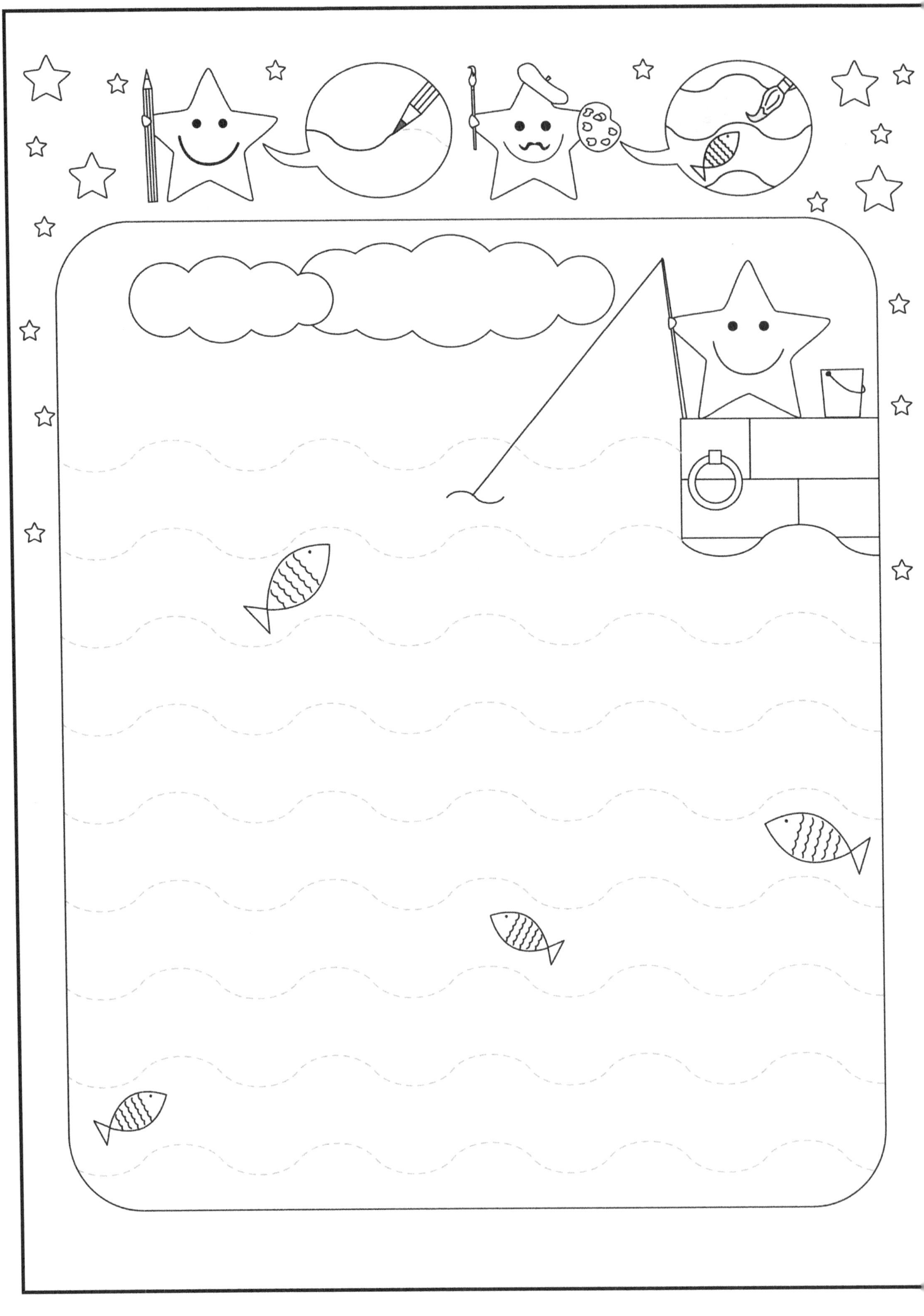

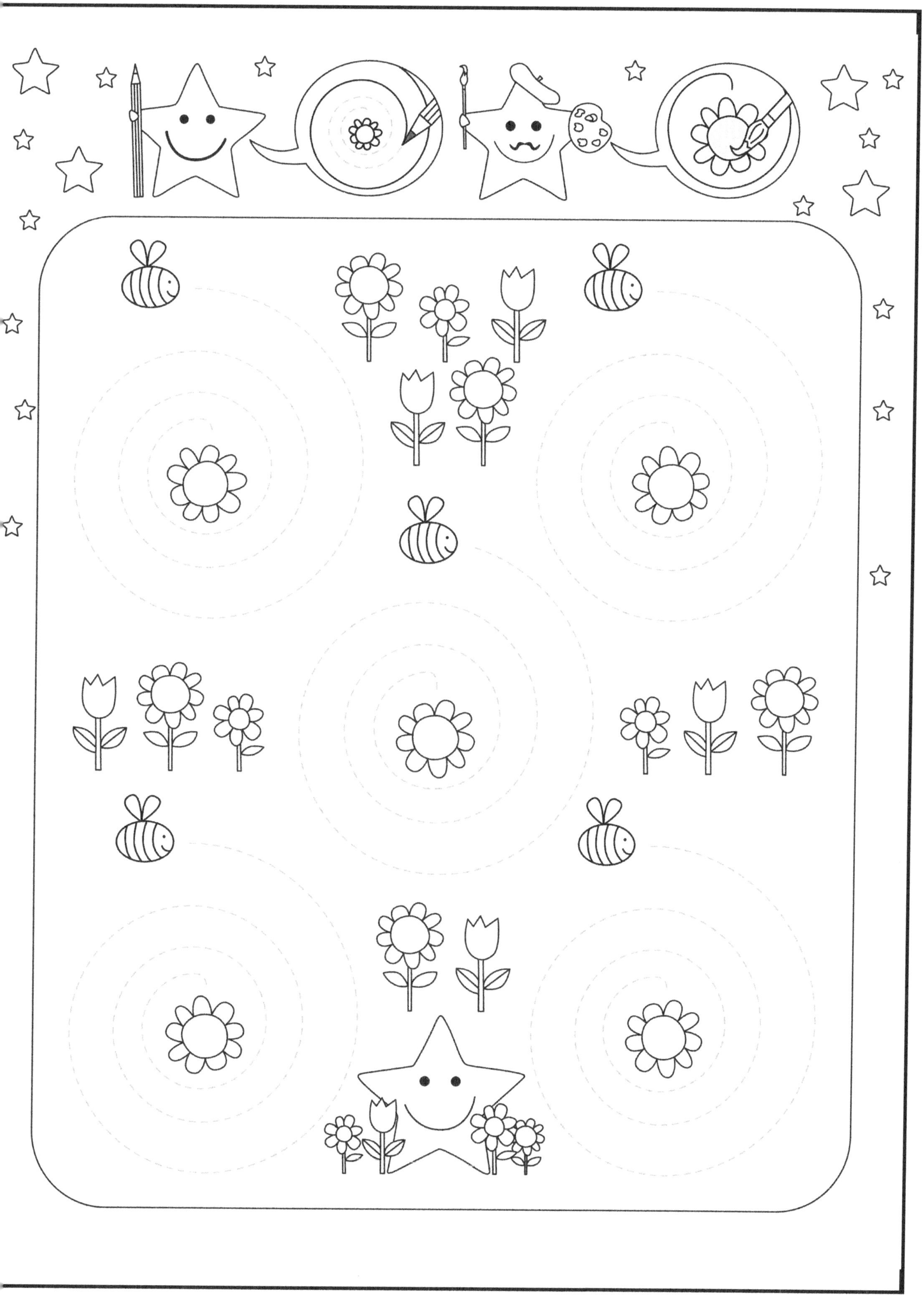

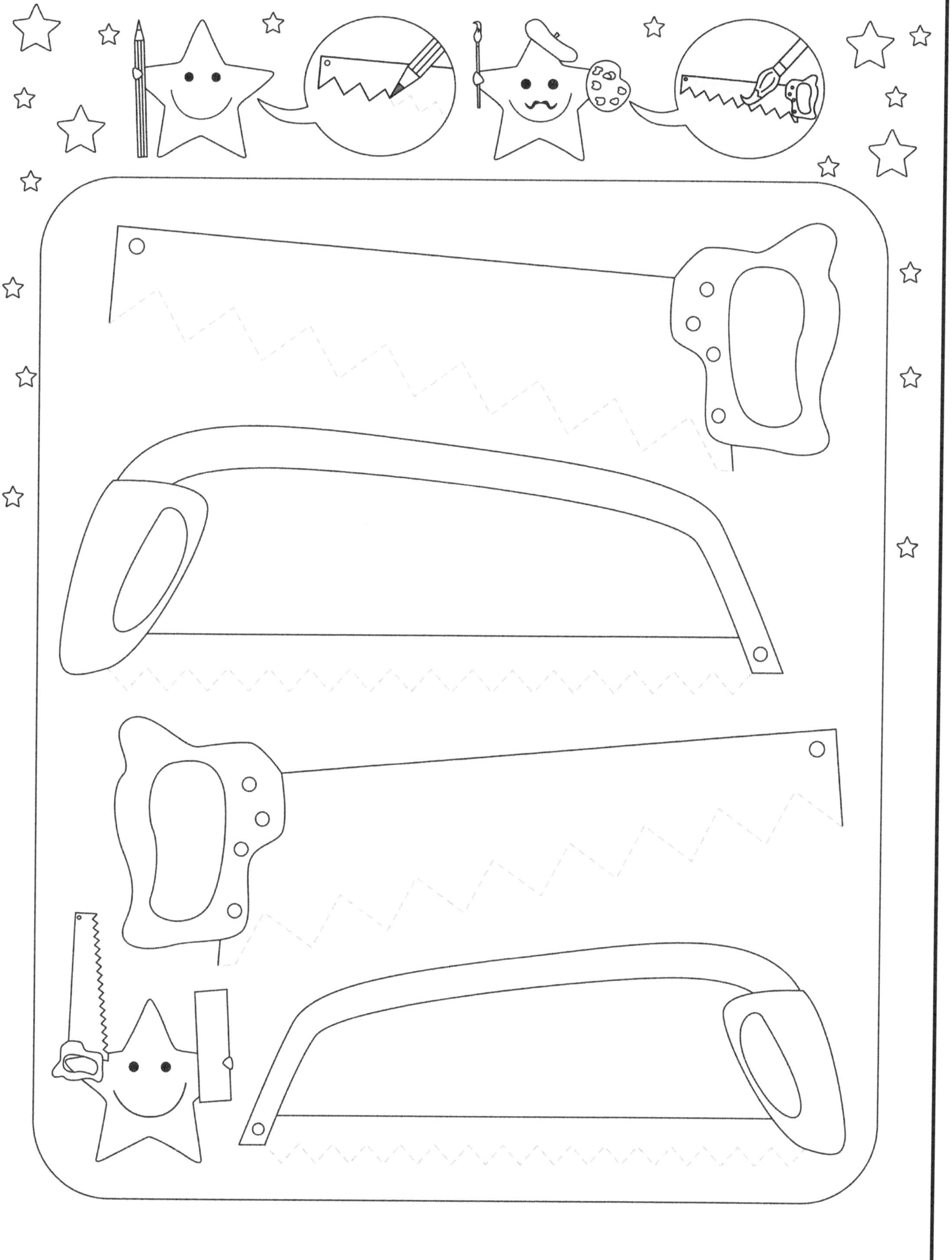

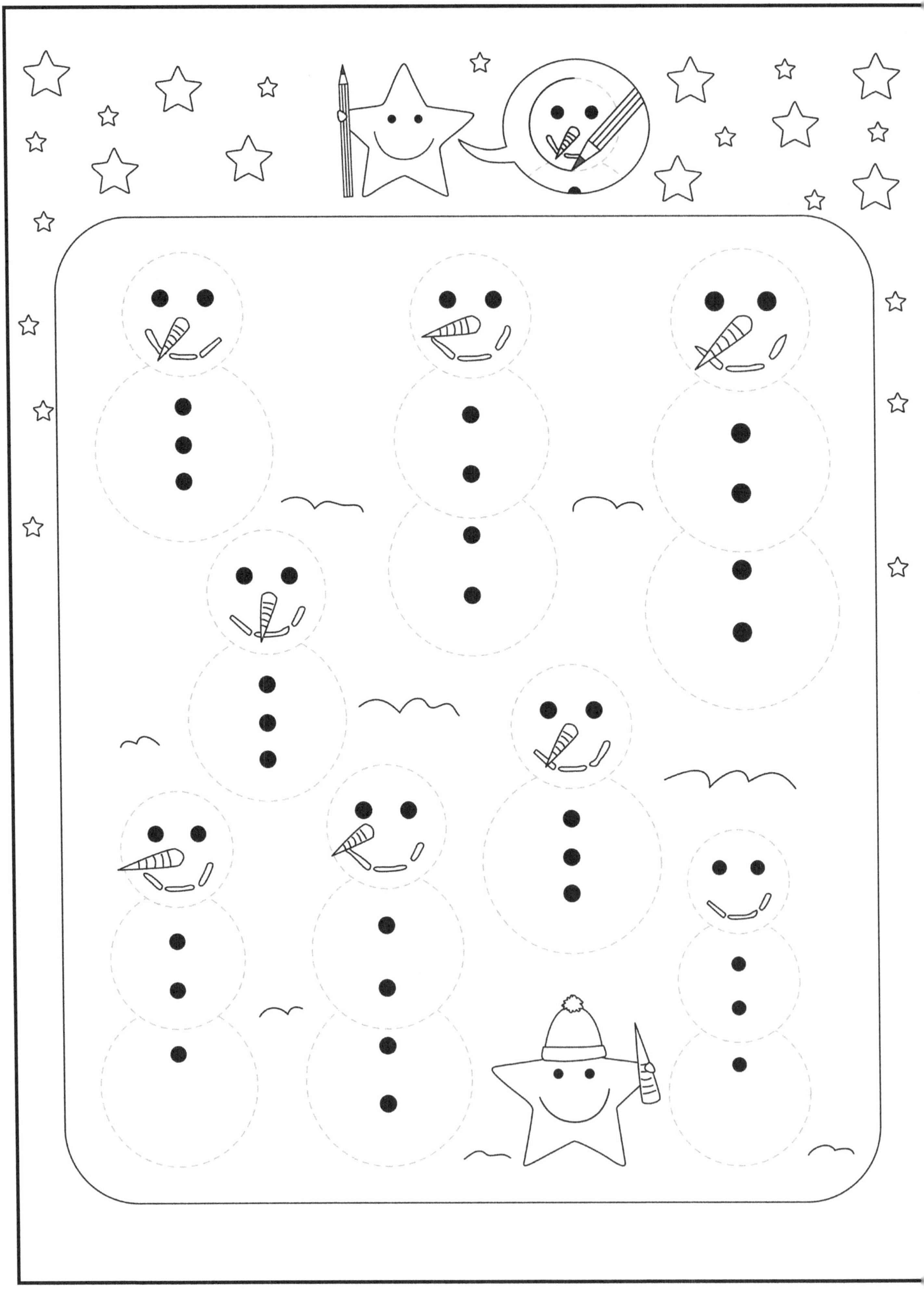

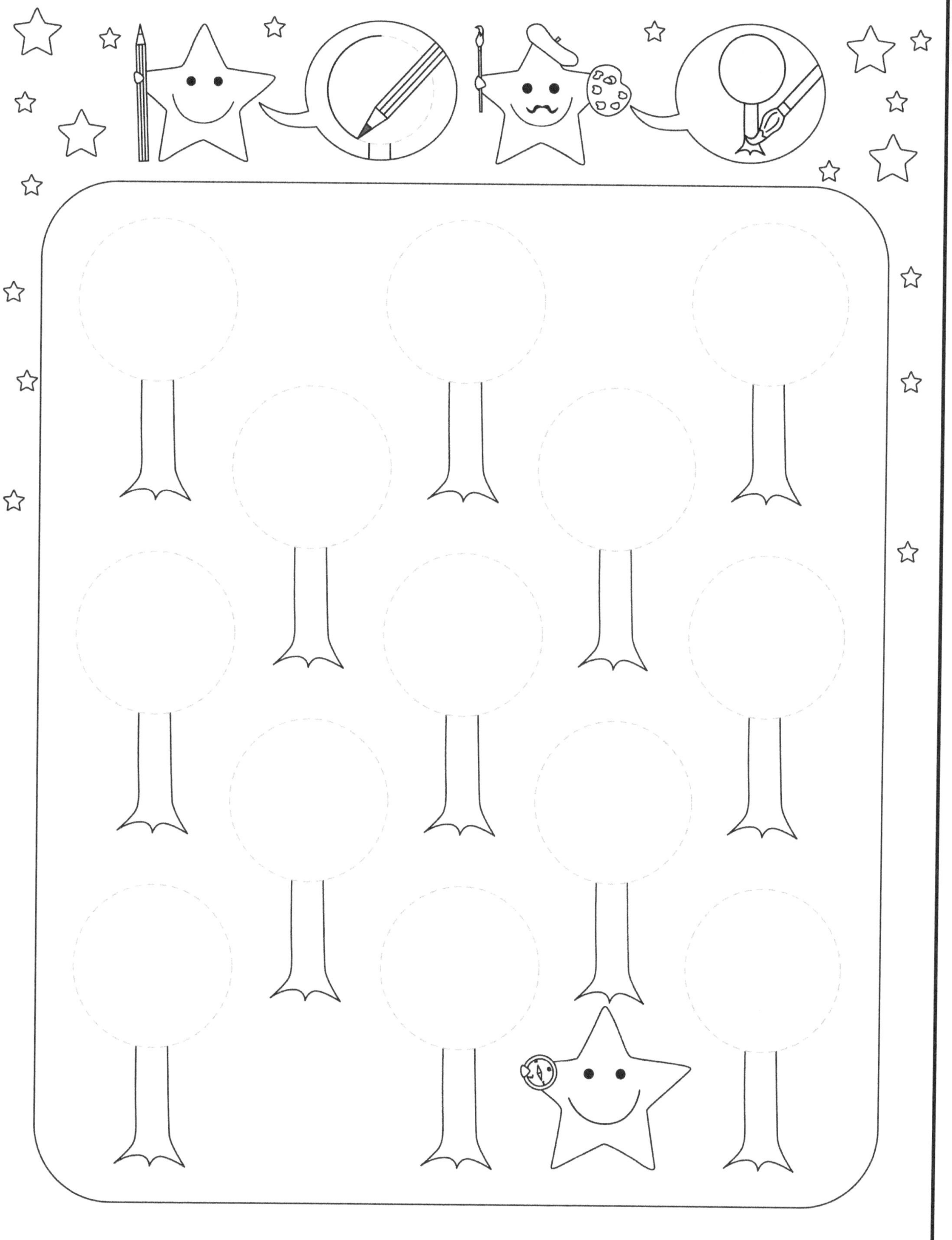

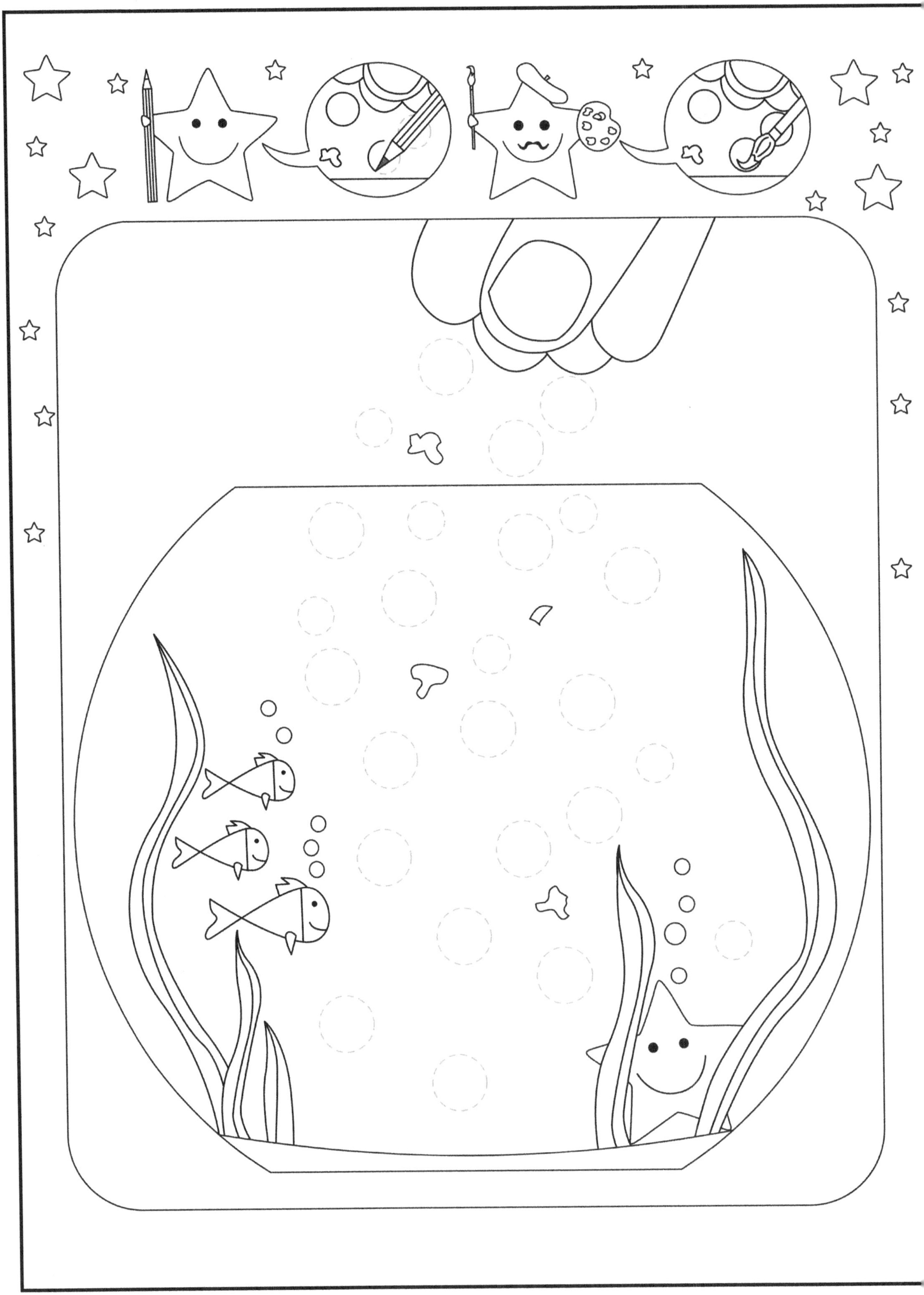

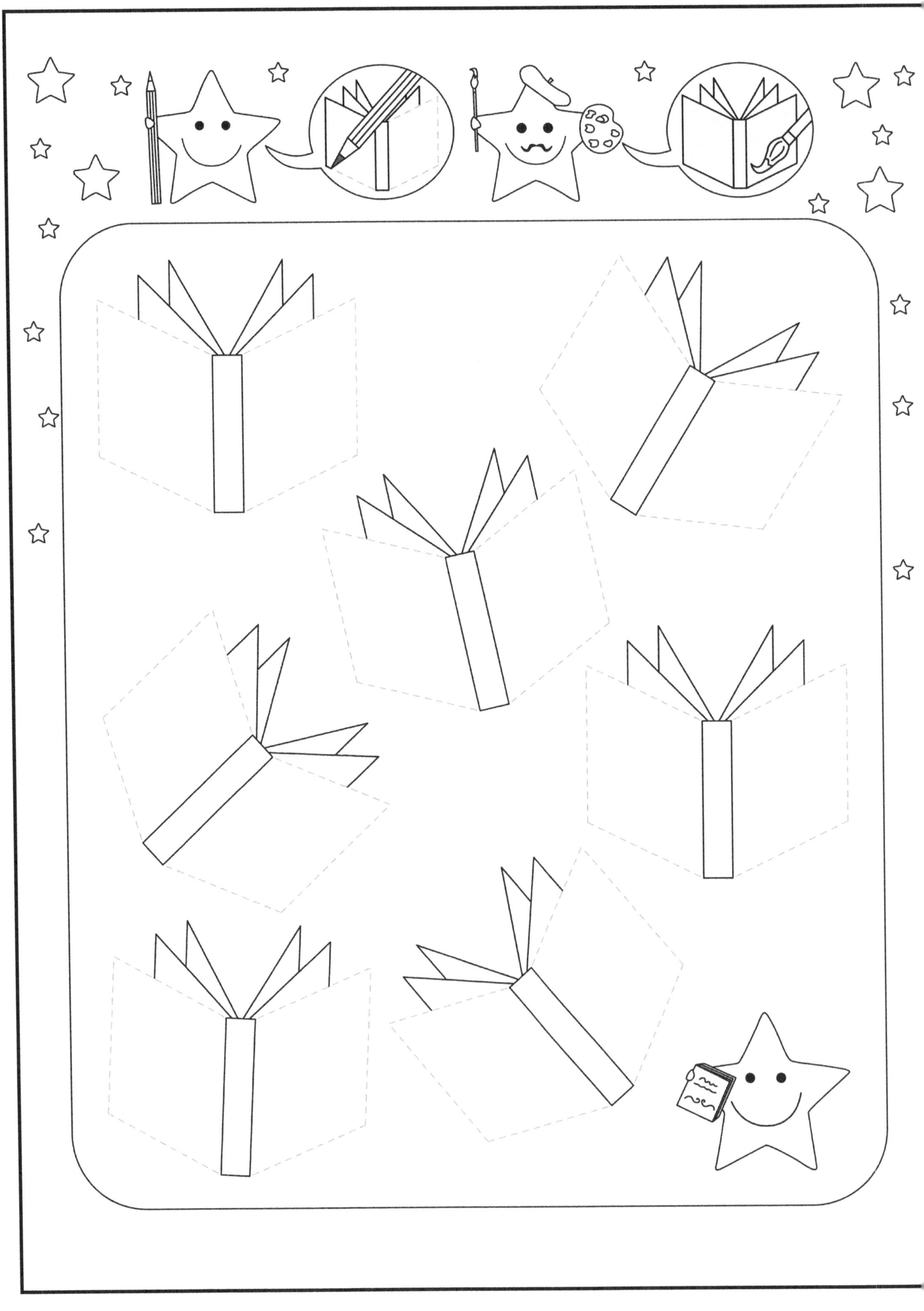

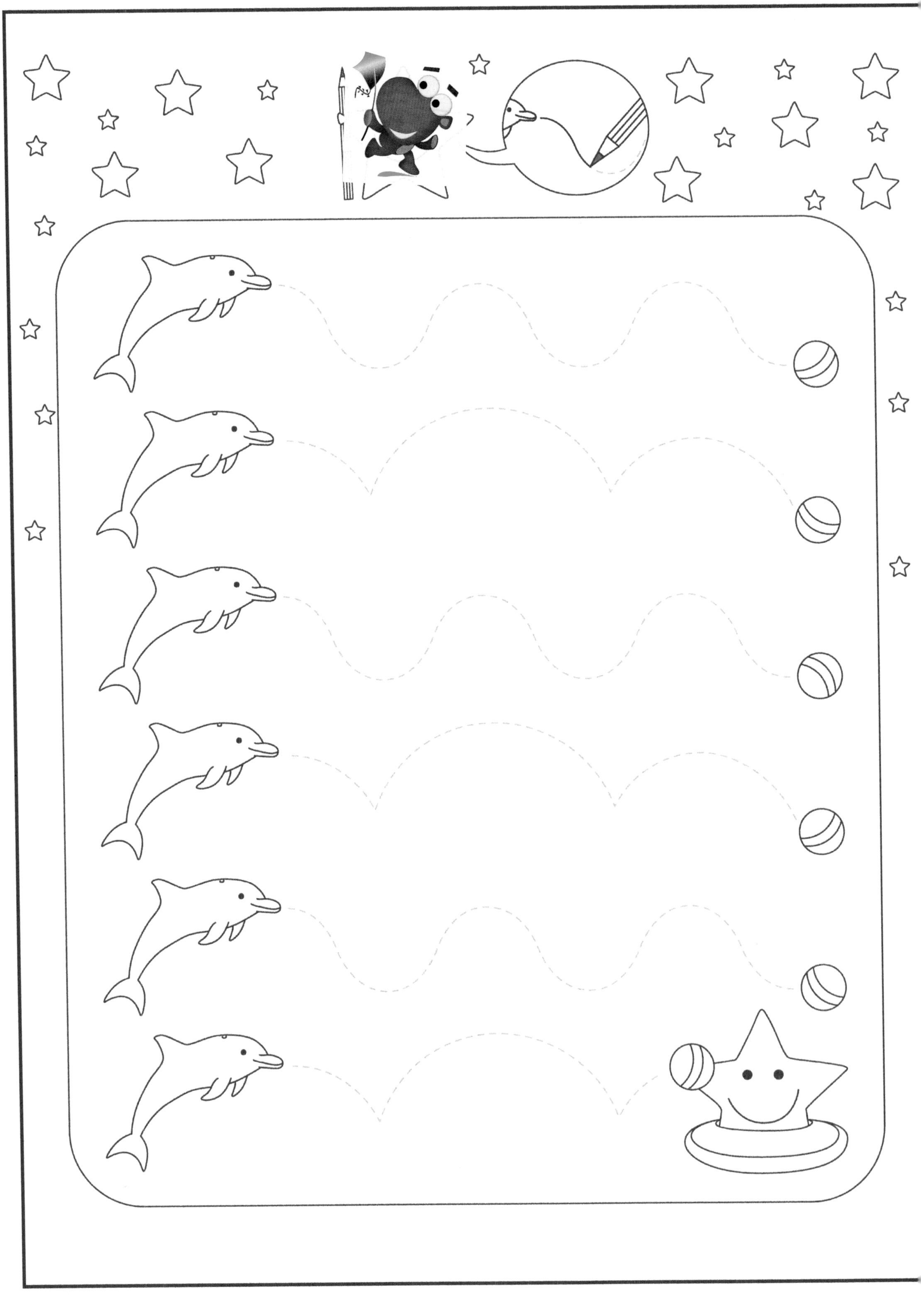

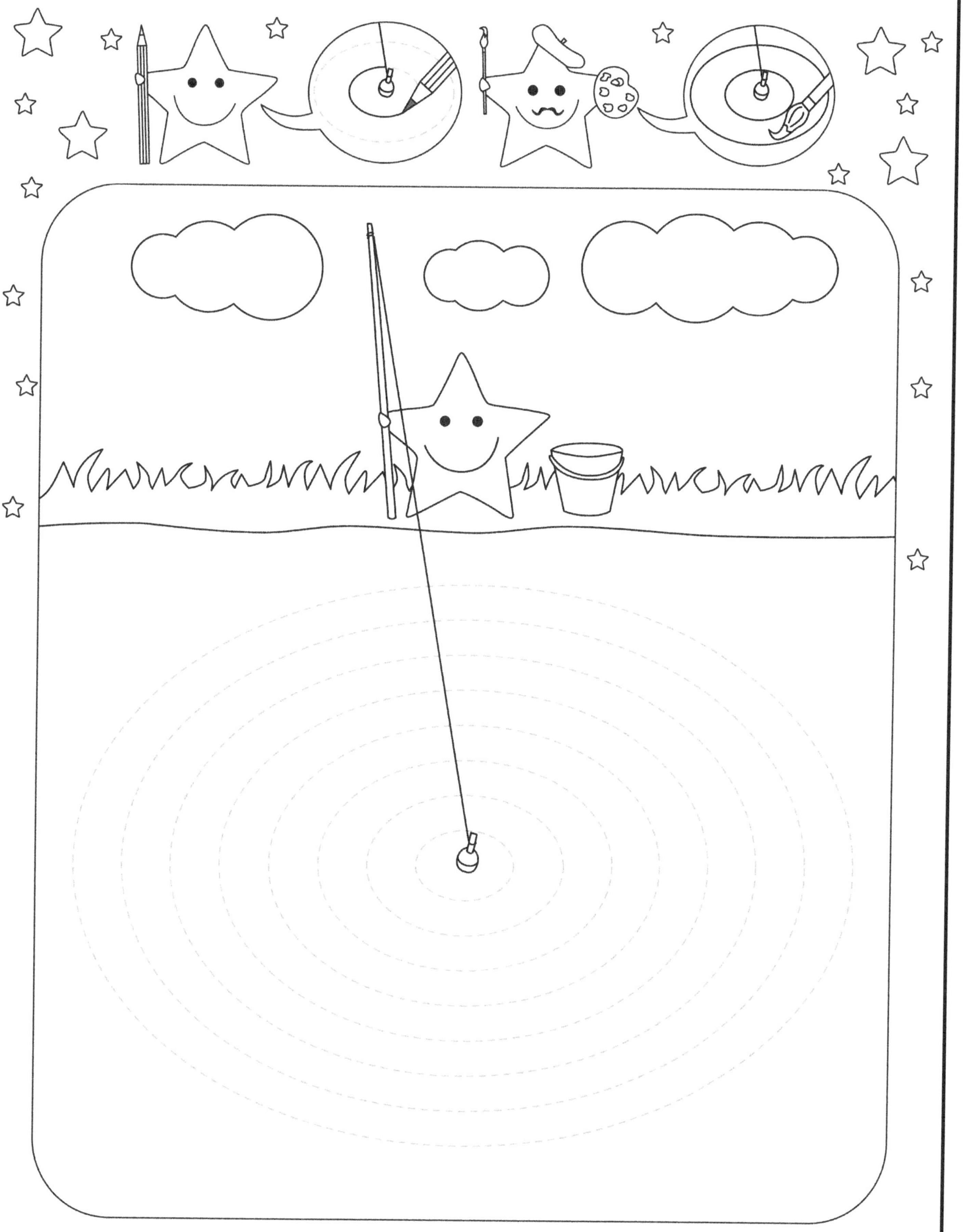

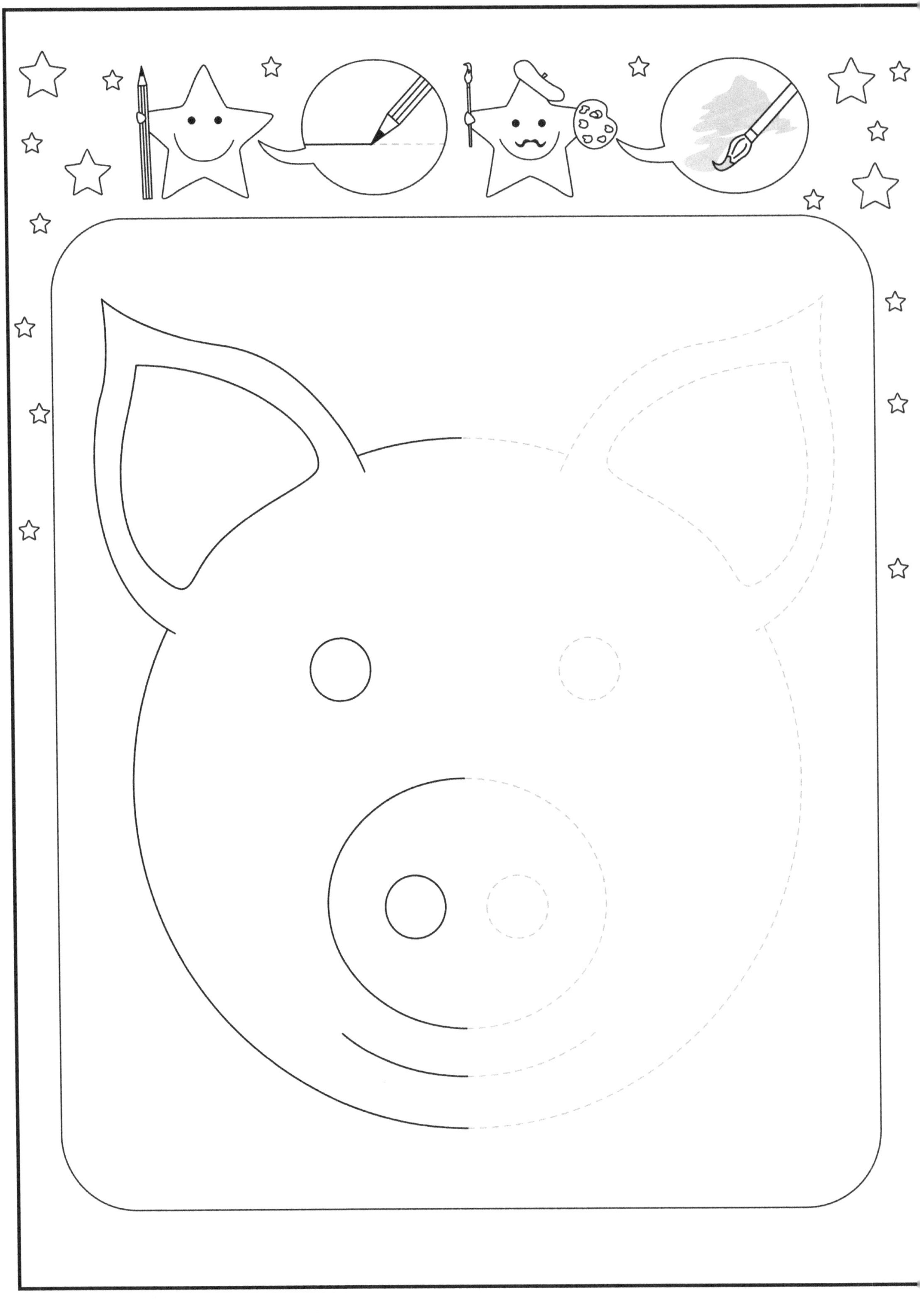

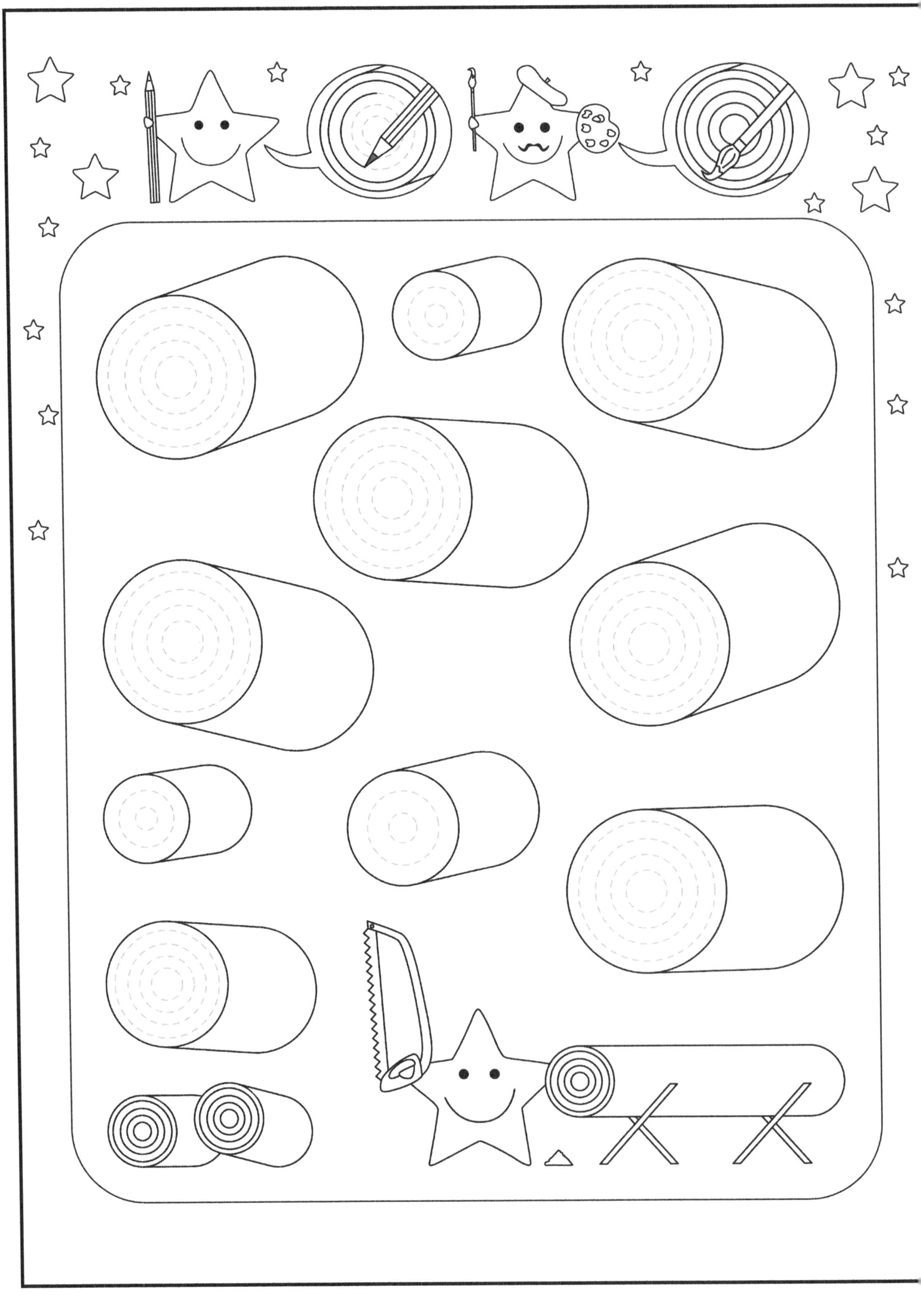

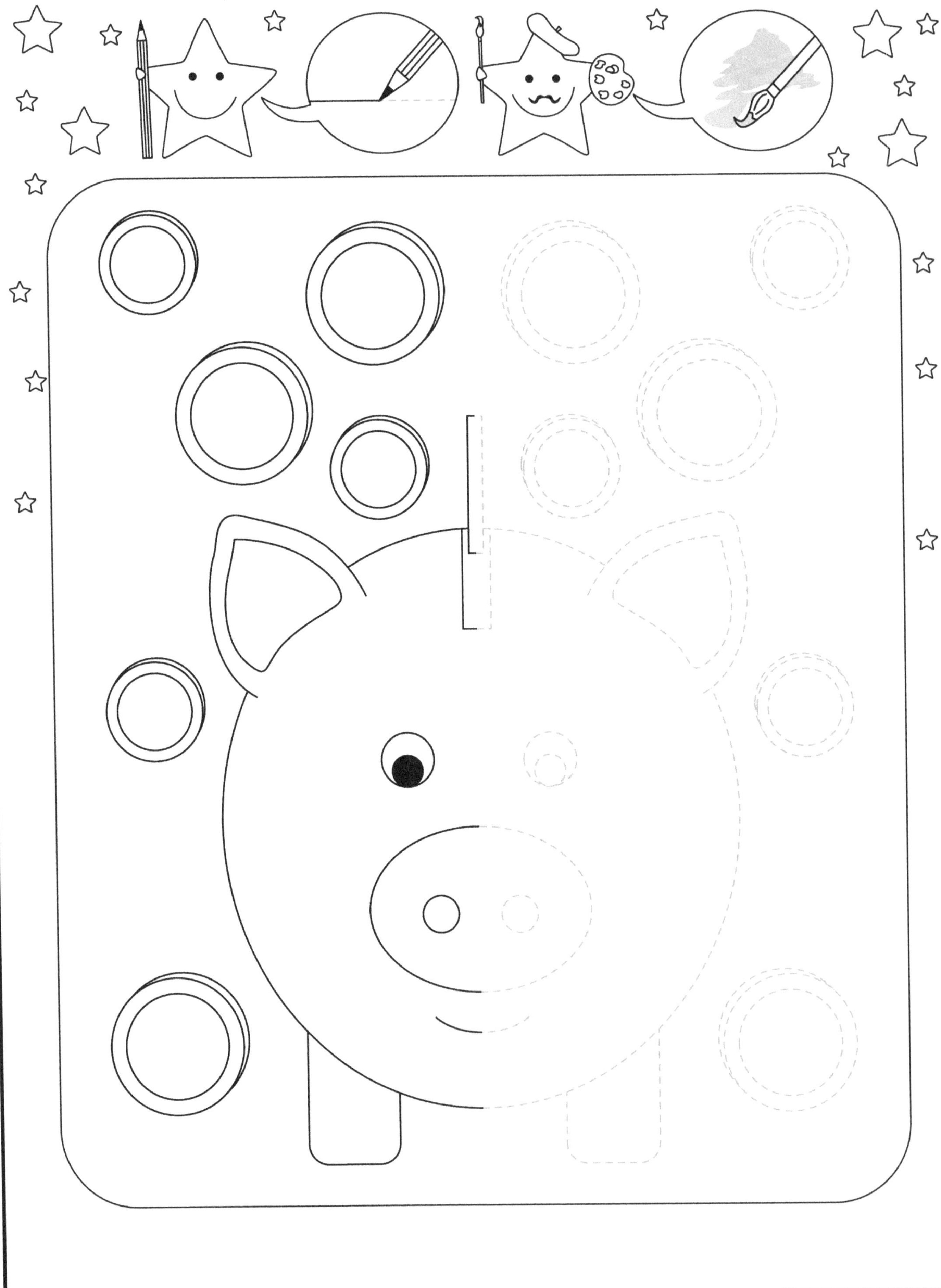

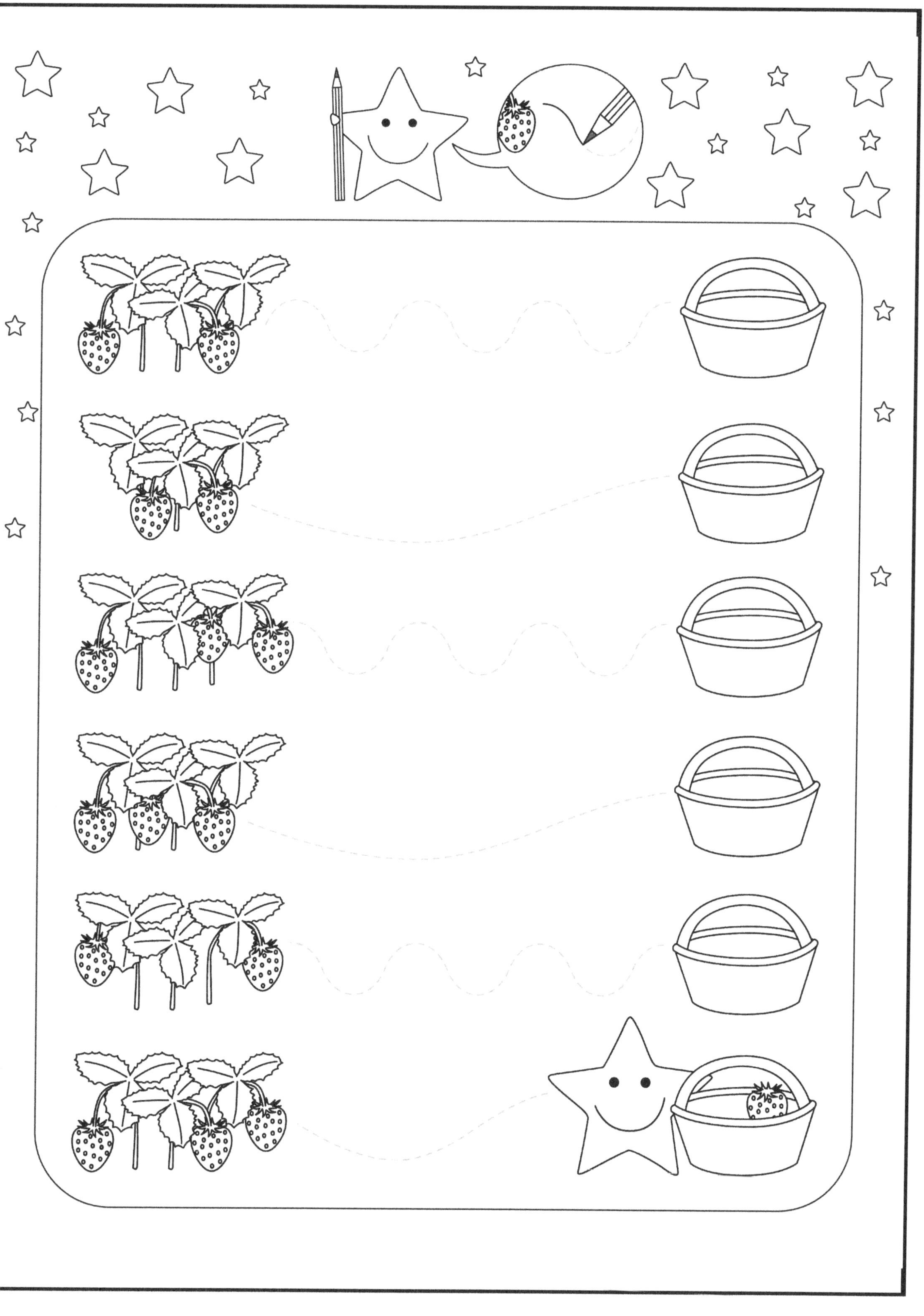

Trace & Color the Shapes

CIRCLE

SQUARE

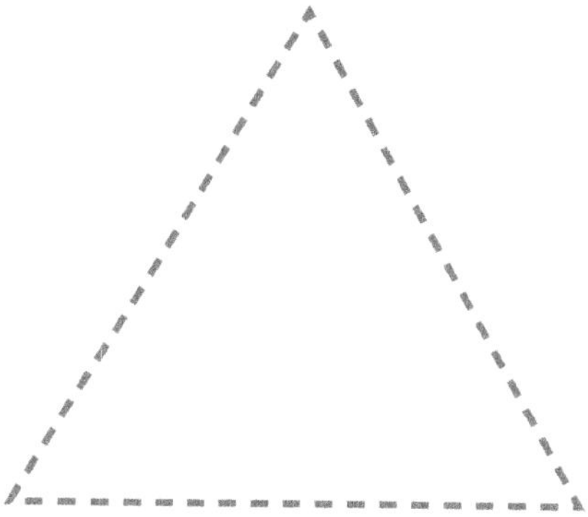

TRIANGLE

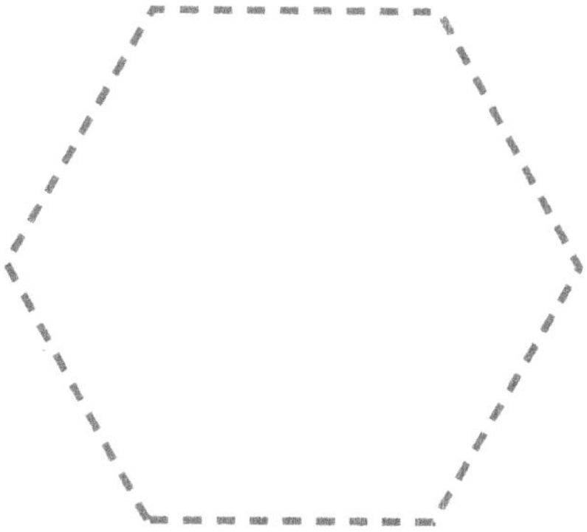

HEXAGON

RECTANGLE

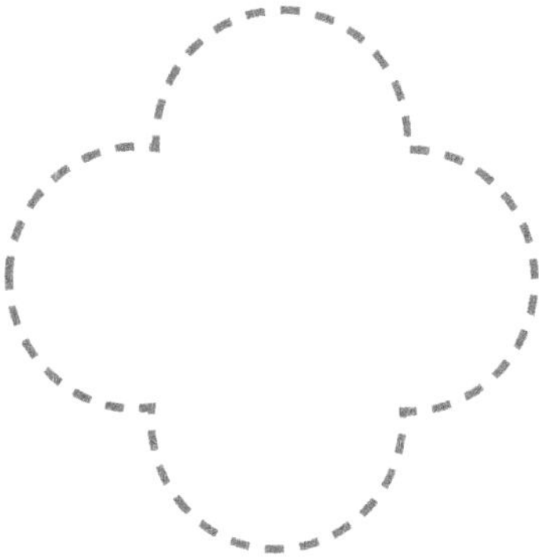

QUATREFOIL

STAR

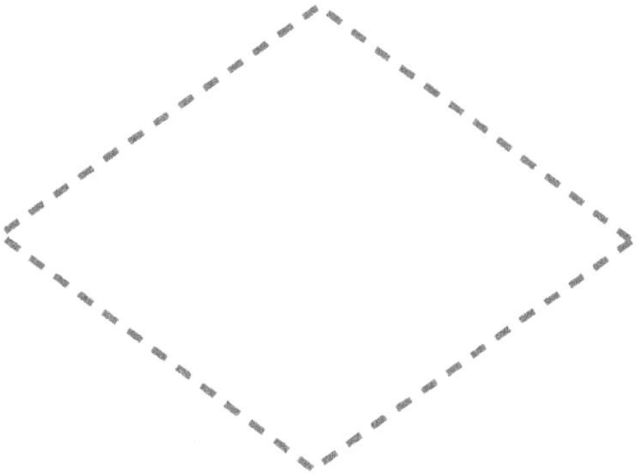

DIAMOND

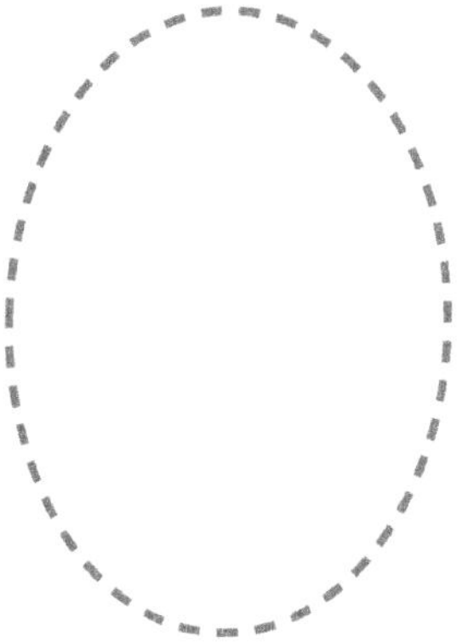

OVAL

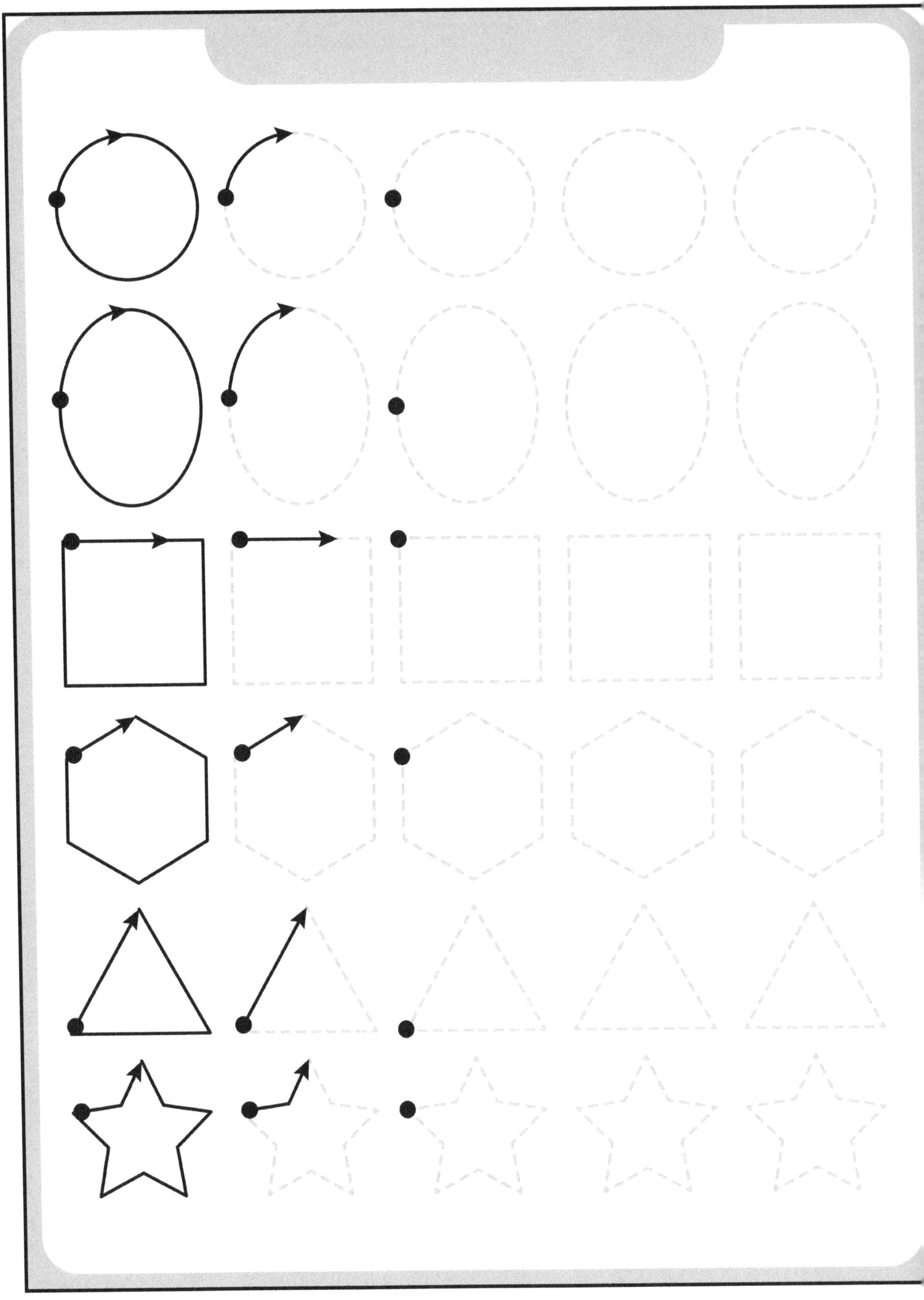

Trace the Shapes

37169007R00038

Made in the USA
Middletown, DE
22 February 2019